M000203837

THAT'S A GREAT

QUESTION

Provocative Questions. Practical Results.

Greg Bustin

That's A Great Question: Provocative Questions. Practical Results.

Copyright © 2012 Greg Bustin. All rights reserved. No part of this book may be reproduced or retransmitted in any form or by any means without the written permission of the publisher.

Published by Wheatmark®
1760 E. River Rd, Suite 145,
Tucson, Arizona 85718 USA
www.wheatmark.com

ISBN: 978-1-60494-671-0 (paperback)
ISBN: 978-1-60494-672-7 (hardcover)
ISBN: 978-1-60494-673-4 (Kindle)

LCCN: 2011935014

Also by Greg Bustin

Lead The Way: Charting A Course To Win

Take Charge! How Leaders Profit From Change

Visit www.bustin.com for tools, exercises and
to subscribe to free stuff

For my mother

Roselyn Gliddon Bustin

(April 5, 1928 – February 14, 2011)

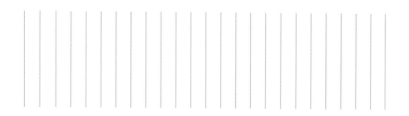

"I went to a bookstore and

asked the clerk,

'Where's the self-help section?'

She said telling me would

defeat the purpose."

George Carlin

"It is better to know some

of the questions

than all of the answers."

James Thurber

Contents

Foreword

There's an old story about a Hollywood producer who's engaged in a conversation, apocryphal I'm sure, but relevant nonetheless. He begins with a one-hour monologue about himself, at which point he says to the other person, "Enough about me, let's talk about you now. What do you think about me?"

It's not a question you'll find in this book.

It would be hard to imagine a better person from a more purposeful vocation to write about the art of asking impactful questions than Greg Bustin. Greg brought his experience as a successful consultant and business owner to Vistage International where he has served as a Chair since 2005 and as a popular Vistage speaker since 2007. My perspective on Greg and the important lessons in this book are offered through that lens.

As a Vistage Chair, asking provocative questions isn't just something Greg does, it's part of who he is. Yet he's constantly honing his craft. In one-to-one leadership development sessions with CEOs and key executives, Greg helps leaders explore and discover their own paths to professional success and personal fulfillment. He accomplishes this not by blurting out advice or jumping to conclusions. Rather, he asks probing questions that challenge assumptions and lead people to reach their own conclusions. As a result, they *own* the solution, which is far better than skeptically following or perilously rejecting a consultant's "do this!" advice.

Asking probing questions of individual leaders can be challenging enough, but Greg also knows how to inspire a group of CEOs to ask good questions of one another and of their staffs. It's an essential component of the Vistage peer advisory experience and among the key reasons leaders invest their time in this extraordinary setting. The questions that are posed and the outcomes of the exchange generate deeper understanding, new ideas and better decisions.

What's more, Greg never stops asking questions of himself. He understands the difference between questioning yourself and asking yourself hard questions – questions that serve to clarify our real goals, strengthen our resolve, and give our activities and lives purpose.

Of course, understanding the benefits of asking questions is one thing, but the "art" of asking those questions is where you'll glean the practical value in Greg's book. Here's where his experience shines through. You'll not only find hundreds of provocative questions that can lead you to practical results, you'll also learn some of the secrets to crafting questions that are inviting, not threatening. As we know, a question that's poorly framed can incite defensiveness. Greg shares with us ways to ask questions that draw a person into a meaningful, impactful conversation.

Greg guides us to see that asking the right questions is critical for uncovering the root causes of problems and gaining confidence in proposed solutions. The art of question-asking is critical for leadership, particularly of businesses. A leader should not be expected to have all the answers and can be forgiven for occasionally having the wrong answers. But asking the questions that penetrate to the heart of the matter is a leader's obligation and, in fact, one of a leader's most significant contributions.

At Vistage, we've been privileged to benefit from Greg's wisdom for a number of years. As a Chair and as a speaker, he has touched the lives of our members – and the thousands more whom they influence. He has demonstrated how and he's inspired them to be better leaders who make better decisions and achieve better results. From this book, you too can learn the art and value of question-asking from a master practitioner.

I'll end with another Hollywood story, The Wizard of Oz. As you may recall, Dorothy ultimately discovers she didn't need someone to take her back to Kansas after all. She had the power all along to go home any time she wanted. Who knows? Maybe if someone had asked Dorothy a few great questions about those shoes she was wearing she would have gotten home much sooner.

~ Rafael Pastor
Chairman of the Board and Chief Executive Officer
Vistage International

Acknowledgements

Any book, my friend Tim Law says, is a compilation of previous thought. This book certainly is.

So while it's impossible to list everyone to whom I'm indebted, these people stand out as having helped me think differently and ask better questions, including...

Bill Case, who recruited me to become a Vistage Chair.

David Belden, who first challenged me in Chair "boot camp" and continues to enlighten.

Ole Carlson, who helped me think differently and continues to inspire me.

Larry Wilson, who first asked me the two most difficult questions.

Bob Berk, who reminded me to always be curious.

Heather Anderson, Ed Coriell, Allen Hauge, Garth Jackson and Mike Murray, who each inspired at least one great question in this book.

Larry Hart, who reminded me that less is more.

Steve Elson, who shared, among other wisdom, the seven judgmental words.

Iain Lindsay, who championed my first speaking engagements in England and Wales, and shared his enthusiasm, experiences and exercises.

Julian Cook, whose term "stiletto moment" vividly describes the power of a great question.

Mike Donahoe, who modeled the role of a coach in our one-to-one coaching sessions.

Arthur Eisenberg and his team, who provided design and direction.

Jeff Travis and Greg Carr, who kept me out of the ditches.

Rafael Pastor, who leads those who lead leaders.

The men and women of Vistage International, whose efforts help those who help leaders.

Each of the Vistage Chairs around the world who invited me to speak to their groups: I learned something from each of you and your members.

Friends and fellow Vistage Chairs in Dallas-Fort Worth – Larry Hawks (our champion), Brant Houston (our leader), Nina Atwood, John Beatty, David Boyett, Jim Eckelberger, Chas Humphreyson, Mike Richards, Lonnie Smith, Nancy Starr, Ken Stibler, Mark Winters – who provide perspective and support.

The men and women of my three Vistage groups – CE 3211, CE 3357 and Key 9107 – who allow me to work with them and who teach me something new every time we're together.

My clients, whose confidence in me is gratifying and whose minds are open to learning.

And, most important, to my wife Janet and daughter Jordan. Janet believed in and encouraged this book from the very beginning, and then she and Jordan provided lots of love, support and help as well as the oft-asked question, "What's for dinner?"

Introduction

"In all affairs it's a healthy thing now and then to hang a question mark on the things you have long taken for granted."

Bertrand Russell

"That's a great question," the CEO said.

The two of us were sitting in his office and we were in the middle of our monthly coaching session.

It was a stiletto moment. I'd pierced the heart of the CEO's issue, and now he was feeling a bit queasy.

Over time, I've learned to appreciate the enormous power questions wield. Early in my consulting career, I was expected to answer questions for my supervisors and clients. Later, when I was running an office and, eventually, my own firm, I saw the value a single question brought to thorny issues, strained relationships and difficult decisions.

These days, I work exclusively with executives to help them and the organizations they lead improve their performance. At this writing, I've led more than 150 strategic planning sessions for companies of all sizes in dozens of different industries, run nearly 200 leadership workshops throughout the U.S., Canada and Europe, and conducted more than 1,600 executive coaching sessions with senior executives of Fortune 500 companies and owners of small and mid-sized companies. Questions have formed the backbone of all of these engagements.

I believe the "great question" comment from those on the receiving end of a pointed question is a reflexive response. The response can be offered as a compliment to the inquisitor in the hope of getting off the hook. Sometimes, it's uttered to buy time and establish permission for not answering quickly, crisply or convincingly. And occasionally, it's in recognition that a worthy challenge has been laid down around an issue that previously was not considered or conveniently ignored.

Whatever the reason, I hear that "great question" phrase frequently.

The question I'd posed to the CEO may not have been one of the truly *great* questions of all time, but it was nevertheless an *insightful* question because it caused him to confront from a different perspective a tough issue he'd been wrestling with for some time.

So there we were – the CEO and me – in his office. He was thinking. I was waiting for his response.

After about 30 seconds of silence that felt more like 30 minutes, the CEO said the words I was waiting to hear.

"I hadn't really looked at it from that perspective," he said. He then made a decision and told me the action he would take based on having considered the issue from a fresh perspective.

That's the power of a great question. It provides an opportunity to ponder issues that may have been taken for granted, never considered or purposefully ignored. It allows us to think differently about those issues. And then prompts us to dig deeper to expose – within ourselves and within others – what's most meaningful.

We go through life asking and answering millions of questions. We ask them of ourselves, our loved ones, colleagues and customers, suppliers and strangers. In many cases, our questions are posed because we want information. *Where is the train station? How much is that? Have they had their baby yet? When will the shipment arrive? Will we meet our forecast this quarter?*

Those are good questions.

The questions you'll find in this book, however, are different. What you'll find here are thought-provoking questions that can unlock and open new doors for you. The vast majority of the questions are framed from a business perspective because that's where most of the people I work with are focused. But the reality is I'm hired by business executives and then human beings show up. So you'll also find plenty of questions about personal matters that inform and influence business decisions.

We'll also examine how to ask great questions. And we'll look at words that, when used in questions, often trigger undesirable responses.

When I told my daughter Jordan that I was compiling a collection of questions, she asked, "Will you provide the answers?" "How could I?" I responded. "The answers to each of these questions is personal."

There are hundreds of so-called self-help books that provide step-by-step guidance on how to address just about every issue under the sun. I've written books like those, too.

This book is intended to help you think about what really matters to you.

After all, the quality of our lives is determined by the power of the provocative questions we're willing to ask ourselves.

And though you won't find every question you'll need on life's journey, you will find some of the most penetrating questions I've asked to help very successful people get more of what they want out of life.

Why Questions Matter

"In the book of life, the answers
aren't in the back."

Charlie Brown

We can learn from children.

They ask questions all the time. Unexpected questions. Tough questions. Perplexing questions.

Children seem to have an unlimited source of questions.

Children are relentless questioners. Their curiosity is compelling. And they're fearless. They'll ask anything, including the awkward question. Yet they ask their questions with a pureness of heart and a desire to understand and learn that adults would do well to emulate.

Because somewhere along their way to adulthood – typically in the early years of school – children actually learn to ask fewer questions and, instead, begin to memorize the answers that have been handed to them. Children learn that asking questions can get you laughed at. *"What a stupid question!"* Children learn that asking questions reveals a lack of understanding. *"He doesn't get it!"* Children learn that asking questions slows everyone down in our fast, faster, fastest get-it-done-now world.

So by the time kids grow up to become adults and enter the workforce, the curiosity that was so compelling a few years earlier has been stifled. Caution has replaced fearlessness. Memorization has replaced thinking. And the ability to master the science and art of asking questions is rarely exercised.

Answers are important. The right answers propel people, businesses, schools, churches and governments to new levels of success.

Yet more often than not, the best answers come from great questions.

The Power of Questions

When Peter Drucker died in 2005, Jack Welch, former chairman of General Electric Co. and regarded as one of the most successful business leaders of his time, called Drucker "the greatest management thinker of the last century."

Drucker was a master at posing the deceptively simple question that could unlock potential.

Early in Welch's new role as CEO of GE, he invited Drucker to the company's headquarters. Drucker posed two questions to Welch that shaped the CEO's long-term strategy: *"If you weren't already in a business, would you enter it today?" "And if the answer is 'No,' what are you going to do about it?"*

These two great yet simple questions prompted Welch to insist that every GE business be either No. 1 or No. 2 in its class. If they were not, the business was fixed, sold or closed. The strategy that transformed GE into one of the most successful American corporations of the past 25 years started with two questions posed by Drucker.

One of Drucker's guiding principles was the belief that *"What everybody knows is frequently wrong."*

Whether or not you agree with this premise, consider the impact of leading a team or an organization where questions go unanswered or – worse – unasked.

First, a reluctance to ask a question diminishes confidence. If you fear embarrassment from asking a so-called dumb question, you'll reach a point where you choose to remain silent. The flip side of this coin is a reluctance to admit you don't know the answer to a question. Either way, this kind of fear imprisons you and eventually puts a major dent in your self-esteem. This kind of fear also likely places a ceiling on your career.

Second, a reluctance to ask a question hinders individual and organizational performance. How many times have you left a meeting where the purpose of the meeting, the decisions made in the meeting and the next steps coming out of the meeting were fuzzy? Asking questions brings clarity to purpose, decisions and tasks. *What do we want to accomplish? Who will do what by when?* If those issues are not clear, the chances of an assignment getting done well, on time and on budget are reduced.

Third, a reluctance to ask a question hinders intellectual growth. Life is not a multiple choice exam, so those in the workplace are well-advised to learn that the way a question is asked often determines the quality and practical application of the answer. What's more, when questions are asked, those on the receiving end of the question learn just as much – about a situation, themselves, and the person posing the question – as the questioner. Asking questions improves listening skills, strengthens problem-solving abilities and fosters innovation.

Fourth, a reluctance to ask questions hinders teamwork. High performing teams are built on a foundation of trust. It's easier to ask the tough, necessary question if you're confident the people around the table have each other's best interests and the best interests of the organization in mind. Questions promote self-awareness and create a professional framework for resolving conflicts. Are the questions being asked in your organization posed to learn or to judge?

Fifth, a reluctance to ask questions hinders organizational growth. I've seen the so-called dumb question unlock an organization's potential or fix a problem that adds hundreds of thousands of dollars of profitability. Asking questions allows a problem or opportunity to be considered from a fresh perspective. It's staggering to think where some of the organizations

I've worked with would be if the obvious question had not been asked. A questioning organization is a growing organization – it encourages questions, challenges assumptions, learns from experiences, and embraces the type of positive change that allows it to outperform itself, not just its peers.

Asking vs. Doing

Leaders are problem-solvers. When leaders see a problem, they work to identify a solution and then execute.

When this behavior occurs in an organization, three things are happening and two of them are bad.

The good thing that's happening is that the potential problem is being avoided or an actual problem is being corrected.

But this approach stifles personal development.

And it strangles organizational growth.

When you rush to rescue a colleague who's pursuing a course of action that may not produce the desired results, you're limiting their independent problem-solving ability because your colleague thinks, *"Well, I guess that's what my boss really wants me to do..."*

As the leader, you're short-circuiting your colleague's ability to assess the issue, develop questions and select a solution. In the long run, you're hijacking their ability to perform at a higher level and grow to their full potential.

So the next time a colleague comes to you and asks, *"What do you think I should do?"* turn the question back to them and ask them what they think.

Not all of your colleagues' decisions will turn out to be correct. The same is true for you, too, right?

That's okay. Mistakes are going to happen. "If you're not making mistakes," said coaching legend Vince Lombardi, "you're not trying hard enough."

Mistakes are the inevitable by-products of any leader's decisions.

Yet in a high-performing organization that accepts some failure as a component of improvement and growth, there's a collective trust among employees who understand that questions – especially tough questions – will be welcomed, asked and answered before decisions are made and after results are produced.

Growth, after all, comes from asking great questions. So unleash your inner kid.

How to Use This Book

"It is a riddle, wrapped in a mystery, inside an enigma."

Winston Churchill

Life is a riddle.

Actually, it's a never-ending series of riddles. We're not expected to solve every one of them, but we should solve some of the more significant ones and have fun along the way.

The 18 topics examined in this book are, year after year, the most compelling areas the successful people I work with examine regularly. You'll find more than 500 questions in this book that have been selected from more than 3,000 questions. Each question represents an opportunity for you to gain insight, unlock potential and move toward a desired result.

You may know that *quest* is the root of *question*, from the original Latin word *quaerere*, which translates as "to hunt, search or seek." *Quest* is believed to have been first spoken in the 14th century, so you may picture knights on horseback in their search for the Holy Grail. Today, when we ask questions of others, we seek information. When we ask questions of ourselves, we may be searching for our personal Holy Grail – that elusive prize of self-knowledge.

Which brings us to how you can use this book.

Provocative questions

First, use this book for yourself. Answer the questions you find here as part of a process to help you determine what's important to you.

Second, use this book as a guide with your colleagues at work to help your team zero in on things that matter to your department, your division or to the entire business enterprise. You may also choose to use the book with family members, boards of for-profit and not-for-profit organizations, clients, and any other group that you believe would benefit from answering thought-provoking questions that help sharpen purpose, affirm values and drive results.

I suggest you start by yourself, beginning with the chapter examining Purpose. After that, feel free to skip around.

If you agree that it makes sense to begin with this book as I've suggested, consider investing a bit of time and money to change your surroundings, isolate yourself and get off to a good start. You might decide to take a train trip over a weekend. Or check into a luxury hotel for a one-person mini-vacation. What about a stroll along the sea shore, a hike on a mountain trail or a walk in the country to free your mind, get your heart pumping and your creative juices flowing?

So while going away is not mandatory, finding solitude for reflection is.

For your quiet time alone with this book, bring paper, blank journals, PostIt Notes™, pencils and pens in an array of colors. I strongly encourage you to move through this book the old-fashioned way and not the 21st century way with a laptop or PDA by your side. You should be focused on the questions – and your personal quest – and not the device that will surely distract your thinking with interruptions. You'll get more out of this book and, more important, out of yourself.

Whatever course you follow, expect your initial thoughts to be just that – initial thoughts. Allow your mind to wander. Revel in the thoughts that enter your head as you ponder a smorgasbord of questions about yourself. Capture thoughts before they fly away. Jot down words. Observe patterns. Note and connect similar ideas. Draw pictures. Doodle. All of what you're doing is a natural, valuable and fun part of the process of self-discovery.

Self-discovery doesn't happen overnight or even over a weekend.

Recognize that you'll need multiple sessions by yourself to contemplate these questions in order to fine-tune your thinking and feel confident in your conclusions.

Decide whether it's helpful along the journey of your self-discovery to share some of your answers with loved ones, trusted advisors or your most intimate of friends. Talking out loud from time to time with another person can add clarity to your answers and help you fine-tune your thinking.

Any person that cares about you will be honored to play the role of sounding board, brainstorm resource or accountability partner as you sort through the issues that surface from considering the questions you'll find here.

You shouldn't expect to answer every question in every section in one sitting, nor should you feel it's "wrong" to jump around. With the exception of the first two topics (Purpose and Values) and one of the last (Results), the book is not organized linearly. The questions found in each section are, for the most part, not organized linearly either.

Practical results

My expectations for what you'll get out of this book are twofold: First, that this process will prompt you to think long and hard about issues you've never considered in a meaningful way to help you come to grips with what's really important to you. Second, that you'll use your newfound conclusions to take action in order to get results and enhance your life.

You may also find that revisiting the book – and, more important, your answers – can be helpful in further clarifying your thinking about certain scenarios, issues and opportunities.

This is your book, so make it work for you as you answer some of life's riddles.

Purpose

"All that a man achieves and all that he fails to achieve is the direct result of his own thoughts."

James Allen

Two of the hardest questions any of us must answer for ourselves are "Who am I?" and "What do I want?" So let's jump into the deep end of the pool. Use the thought-starters on the next page to take a long, hard look within yourself to begin answering some of the most difficult and most personally gratifying questions you'll ever face. Fear not: in no time you'll be doing the backstroke.

What is my life's purpose?

What kind of person do I want to be? What obstacles are in my way?

What do I want to do? What obstacles are in my way?

What do I want to have? What obstacles are in my way?

If I could only work on one of the above three – Be, Do, Have – which one would I choose? What's the thought behind my decision?

What do I need? How does what I say "I need" differ from what I say "I want"?

If I stopped today, would it be enough?

How will I know when my purpose has been fulfilled?

What's the biggest thing that I feel is missing in my life?

At a party five years from now, what will I say I've accomplished?

What am I bartering my life for?

Who am I living my life for? Me? Or someone else? Or *something* else?

Why are we in business? What are we trying to accomplish?

What kind of company are we trying to be?

What ideas are we fighting for?

If our company did not exist, what would the world be missing?

What does success look like?

What am I most passionate about today?

Do I want to be rich or king?

How do I keep score?

What gives me a sense of certainty?

I'm on stage accepting a lifetime achievement award for contributions I've made through my work. What is the achievement and what am I saying in my acceptance speech?

If I died today and had written a letter to my loved ones, what would the letter say? Is there anything that's keeping me from writing the letter today?

Values

"Be more concerned with your character than your reputation, because your character is what you really are, while your reputation is merely what others think you are."

John Wooden

Values are the beliefs and ideals that govern our decision-making. Our decisions drive our actions that shape our individual and organizational character. When our values have the potential to cost us something – money, relationships, reputation – our character is put to the test. If we're not really sure what we stand for, we flunk the test every time.

What are my guiding principles?

What are my non-negotiables – the principles or values that I am unwilling to compromise?

We judge ourselves by our intentions but we judge others by their actions. What would it be like if I flipped this perspective?

If I could choose just three words to describe our culture what would those words be? How do these words compare to the ones on our website?

Do our list of company values look like everyone else's ("integrity," "honesty," "respect") or have we articulated them in a fresh way to reflect our company's distinct personality?

How clearly are our values articulated? How well are these values understood by all?

Are our values words on a poster, or do they actually reflect how things get done at our company?

What's one principle I wish everyone practiced?

What happens when behavior does not match our stated values?

If an impartial observer visited our organization, what would that person see, hear and experience? Are we who we say we are?

How would this observed behavior align with or vary from the behavior we desire as an organization? What's causing this behavior?

Can I change my position without changing my principles? What would that look, sound and feel like?

Has there been a time when I paid a price to honor my principles? What price did I pay? Would I make the same decision again?

How do we assess and reward the impact of "soft" indicators like fun, initiative, passion, enthusiasm?

Goal-setting

"What lies behind us and what lies before us are tiny matters compared to what lives within us."

Henry David Thoreau

We are fulfilled when we accomplish something meaningful. We all have dreams. Some of us dream bigger and are more focused about turning those dreams into reality. Setting goals and writing them down brings clarity to our goals and increases the chance that we'll hit what we're aiming for. While life is not a checklist, the first step in getting from Point A to Point B is a well-thought-out roadmap.

If I knew I couldn't fail, what would I do?

How do I describe long-term success? What will my successful company or career *look* like? What will my family life *look* like?

What is the most strategic thing I can attend to in the next 12 months? How will I communicate, measure and execute this initiative?

What do I want to celebrate one year from now? Three years from now?

What would I mourn not accomplishing in the next 12 months? In the next three years? In my life? What steps am I willing to take to prevent this disappointment from occurring?

What will my next 90 days look like?

What happens if I'm hit by the proverbial bus? What's my succession plan? Are my personal affairs in order?

What's my exit strategy? What's my timeframe for exiting?

Where do I want my company or career to be in 3- 5 years? How sure am I of this goal? What will be required to achieve this goal? Where am I the bottleneck?

What concerns do I have as I look to the future? What's my plan to address those concerns?

What is the 800-pound gorilla? Where is my Achilles heel that will make my plan obsolete? What are the three reasons we could go out of business?

Are my expectations appropriate? Have I set the bar too low, too high or just right? If too low, what's caused me to settle? If too high, am I over-reaching?

What is my greatest opportunity that can accelerate my plan?

What business are we really in?

What is it – specifically – that appeals to me about growth? What should our rate of growth be?

What do we do better than anyone else? What empirical proof supports this claim? How can we capitalize on this advantage?

How do I describe what each of these seven areas – the 7 Fs – looks like one year from today?

Faith

Family

Friends

Fitness

Financial

Function (career)

Fun

How do my descriptions change when I view the above categories three years out? Ten years out?

How do I define my own *personal* brand? How do I grow my brand? How do I protect my brand?

Commitment

"Always bear in mind that your own resolution to succeed is more important than any other thing."

Abraham Lincoln

It's hard to be committed if you're not passionate about what you're trying to achieve. So be clear about what you want. And what you don't want. You'll minimize distractions, make better decisions and stay focused on the prize.

What's my definition of commitment?

What am I willing to do – perhaps even to sacrifice – to get what it is that I say I want?

What am I not willing to do?

Are there areas of my life where I am only partially committed (there's an oxymoron) to something I've said that matters to me?

If I approached this commitment as if it really mattered, what would I do? What would I be willing to let go of? Would I be willing to ask for help? What would I be willing to reveal of myself to those who are committed to helping me?

Am I really committed or just going through the motions?

If I exerted just 5 percent more effort, what result would I achieve?

What have I not done that I intended to do? What accounts for the deviation from my plan?

In what other areas of my life where I've given my word am I not delivering on my promise – to myself and to others?

If I feel any reluctance to make a commitment, to what root cause can I trace this condition?

Am I modeling the commitment that I want to see from others?

Organizations strive to keep their promises to customers. How well do we keep the promises we make to one another inside our organization?

How does internal competition show up among departments? Among individuals?

What do I do to gain and follow-up on commitments with my team? If the team members are not making or keeping commitments elsewhere, how do I feel about that? What action do I take?

Trust

"The best way to find out if you can trust somebody is to trust them."

Ernest Hemingway

Trust is the foundation of any meaningful and productive relationship. It's the mortar that cements the bricks on which we build accomplishments. We first must trust ourselves. Once we do, we must then extend our trust to others before we can expect them to trust us.

On a scale of 1 – 10 (with 10 being the best), how would I rate the level of trust in our organization? What factors caused me to rate us the way I did? What changes must we make to increase the trust level in our organization?

On a scale of 1 - 10 (with 10 being the best), how would I rate the level of trust in my personal life? How would those closest to me rate their level of trust in me?

What's the one thing you and I are not talking about that we should be talking about? What's preventing us from having that conversation?

If those that know me best were asked, "What are we not talking about that we should be talking about?" how would they respond?

Is there a time when I've not kept my word? If so, what were the circumstances that prompted my behavior?

Is it possible for me to trust someone too completely? If so, what are the circumstances?

How do I respond when I place my trust in someone and they let me down?

Is how I'm viewing the situation a matter of truth or taste?

What am I kidding myself about?

To what extent do I trust my instincts when making decisions?

When was the last time I showed my vulnerability?

Do I trust my team to do their best every day?

What's one unspoken truth about our organization? About our leadership team? About me? What's preventing people from speaking it?

What do I need most that I am unwilling to ask for help to get?

Communication

"Who you are speaks so loudly I can't hear what you're saying."

Ralph Waldo Emerson

Human beings crave communication. We want it as affirmation, information, instruction and entertainment. Knowing this, we still miss the mark. We provide too little information. Or too much. We communicate the right thing at the wrong time, or the right thing the wrong way. Keep it simple. After all, sometimes we're better communicators when we forget about the words and let our actions do the talking.

How much of my time am I willing to invest to ensure that what's important to me is communicated to those that work for me?

How often do I communicate with the entire organization?

When I communicate, do I take personal responsibility to ensure that what I'm saying is being received the way I intend? How do I do this?

How well do I listen to others? Do I respect their point of view?

Does everyone know what's expected of them to achieve our vision?

Have we clearly defined and communicated the roles of everyone in our organization?

Have we been clear about the implications of organizational and individual success? Of organizational and individual under-performance?

How clearly and consistently have we communicated the rewards and penalties related to individual, departmental, plant/ business unit and organizational performance?

Am I willing to initiate a tough conversation? If I'm hesitant to do so, is it because my expectations were not clear or is something else going on?

How much information am I willing to share? What information am I not willing to share?

Have we developed and deployed a variety of communication vehicles to reflect that people receive and internalize information differently (auditory, visual, kinesthetic, just the facts, creative, etc.)?

If a stranger walked in and asked any employee about our vision, values and strategy, what would they hear?

When was the last time we asked all of our employees for their feedback? What would I hear if I asked them today?

Leadership

"Wherever you see a successful business, someone made a courageous decision."

Peter Drucker

Leadership is not doing what's easy or popular. It's doing what's right and necessary. When things are going well, it's easy to be a leader because it's mostly about managing something – people, projects, deadlines, budgets. But when things go south, it's all about leading people. And making the tough decisions to set things right.

Many great leaders have been forced to overcome difficult obstacles or abandon long sought-after goals. How do I know when to press forward (to rely on my drive, stamina and persistence) and when to change (to accept defeat, adapt and focus on a new goal)?

Who has been the best leader I've encountered in my career? The worst leader? What impact did each have on me? How do I apply this knowledge to my life today?

Who today do I admire? What is it specifically about this person that I admire? Is there anything I can do to build a personal relationship with this person to learn directly from him or her?

Do I behave differently in the office than at home? If so, in what ways? If so, what causes my behavior to differ from place to place?

What's the best business decision I made in the past 12 months? What did I learn?

What's the worst business decision I made in the past 12 months? What did I learn?

What's the biggest missed opportunity of the past 12 months? What did I learn?

What causes me to continue supporting an activity that has not been delivering the results I expect?

What's the most important opportunity I'm facing now?

What are the three most important things I learned today?

What were my top three most significant learning experiences this past month? This past year?

What learning can I pursue in the next 30 days that will help me be more effective?

What one or two things do I believe a leader should not delegate? What causes me to say this?

Would I rather be wrong and happy or know the truth and be uncomfortable? What evidence supports my answer?

What do I do when I am convinced that I am working on the wrong problem?

Am I content to run my company to support my lifestyle or am I trying to accomplish something else?

How would my employees answer if asked what they need in order to be more effective?

What practices (specific, measurable, consistent) will I engage in to enhance my development as a leader? How will I be accountable?

What's the most important decision I'm facing? What's keeping me from making it?

What is the most significant long-term opportunity facing the company? What could I be doing about it this month?

What's the best decision I can make today? If an outsider were to ask that question to my leadership team, how would they answer?

What's the best decision I can make today for five years from now?

Time Management

"The great dividing line between success and failure can be expressed in five words – 'I did not have time.'"

Franklin Field

Time, talent, treasure. Of the three, time is the most valuable because, once spent, it can never be recovered. If that's true, why does it seem that the things we identify as priorities don't get enough of our time? Or how is it that there's never enough time to do something right the first time but there's always enough time to go back and fix it?

Do I spend at least two hours each week thinking about strategy? Am I devoting an appropriate amount of time thinking about ways to improve our performance or grow our revenue?

What am I spending time on? Will this matter one year from now?

Do I prepare a written list of things to do or do I prefer to work from a list inside my head?

What's on my list of things to do that I should give to others that will free me to be my best? To whom will I delegate these activities?

What's the most important thing I can complete this month? Knowing that time usually represents one of the biggest barriers to completing a task – even an important task – what steps am I prepared to take to overcome this barrier?

Does setting a deadline for the completion of tasks increase the likelihood that the task will be completed or does the deadline add another level of stress in my life? If the deadline is causing me stress, is there something else that's at the root of my anxiety?

Do I adjust my own priorities and the priorities of my team to reflect the reality of time or do I adjust my schedule to reflect the importance of my priorities? Where do I start: time management or priority management?

What would I do with an extra eight hours in my week? How can I adjust my schedule to make this happen?

What time of day am I most effective? What would be the impact of blocking an hour each day just for me?

If I tracked my time in 30-minute increments for a month, what would I find? Is this how my time should be spent?

Travel on airplanes provides a rare opportunity for leaders to enjoy uninterrupted time. How do I use my travel time?

What causes me to complete certain important tasks and leave other important tasks undone?

If I charged for my time by the hour (as is customary in some professions), what monetary value would I place on 60 minutes of my time?

If I were a customer or client of my business, would I be willing to pay for the output of my day? If the answer is "no," what action can I take to focus my attention on more valuable activities?

How do we determine the appropriate amount of time to complete a task?

How do we determine that the amount of time invested provides a good return for the outcome produced? Do we calculate this return before we invest the time?

Technology provides continual audio, video and data access to everyone and everything in my world. How do I make time to relax, reflect and re-energize myself? How do I make time for those that matter the most to me?

Rare is the dying person that says, "I wish I'd spent more time at work." What action can I take to allocate more time away from work in order to do more of what I love?

Money

"Money is only a tool. It will take you wherever you want to go, but it will not replace you as the driver."

Ayn Rand

Money is how businesses keep score, and people generally use money as at least one of their benchmarks. Money matters. More to some. Less to others. The following questions will reveal, confirm or change the value you place on making and spending money.

What is the real role of money in my business? In my life?

What are my five most vivid memories about money while growing up? How have these memories shaped me?

What's the monetary implication of doing the things I most enjoy?

What's the monetary implication of doing the right thing?

What's the monetary implication of doing the things that I most dislike?

Should I present and defend my capital strategy to someone other than my banker? When was the last time I did so?

Do I truly know how my banker keeps score? What information is most important to my banker?

Should I present my pricing strategy to someone other than my leadership team? When was the last time I did so?

Do I really know how we make money? Am I crystal clear on why our customers buy from us instead of the competition?

Do our employees know how we make money? Do they understand what it takes to run a profitable business?

How do we deliver value to our customers? Where are our best opportunities to increase our revenue? Where are our best opportunities to increase our profitability?

Where do we get most of our profits? What would happen if we increased our focus on those profitable activities?

What does my personal wealth need to be before I decide it's time to consult a financial planner? What dollar figure would I not be able to say 'no' to?

Do I know what money I require to be happy in retirement? Does my spouse or partner agree? Have I consulted a financial planner?

What would I do if I had no money worries?

Talent + Teamwork

"The secret is to work less as individuals and more as a team. As a coach, I play not my eleven best but my best eleven."

Knute Rockne

The people on your team – in sports, in business, in life – are important because none of us ever accomplishes anything meaningful alone. The talent on your team is the best predictor of your future success. How the stars are recruited, retained and rewarded matters as much as how the under-performers are identified , coached and, barring improvement, terminated.

What's the best team I've ever been a part of? What made it so effective? What can I do to replicate that experience?

Who are five people I spend most of my time with? Are they helping me or holding me back?

What has been my most effective approach to attracting, retaining and engaging people?

Do I know what motivates my team to be their best? How am I using this information?

With what regularity do I ask my colleagues what they need to be more effective?

What's my plan to develop talent? Am I preparing the path for my colleagues, or preparing my colleagues for the path?

What am I doing to help make this job the best job my people have ever had?

Do our employees understand that we'll give them the environment, tools, training and opportunities they need, but that it's up to each one of them to own their respective career?

If I was starting over in my business, which colleagues would I take with me?

What are we doing to encourage the best ideas from the most people?

Am I accepting less from some colleagues than others? What's at the root of my behavior?

Who has the real authority in my business (the ability to say "Yes" and "No")?

Who has the influence?

As I think about my direct reports, how do I rate their effectiveness for the last month? The last quarter? What can I do to help them increase their effectiveness?

How do I feel about someone else getting the credit for my idea?

Are we surprised when people leave our company? Are people surprised when we terminate them?

What is it that makes someone right for our business and right for our organization? Do we have a process for adding talent or does the person hiring a candidate rely on their own experience, system and discretion?

How do we determine the qualifications for the talent we'll need in the future? What's the basis of being a great colleague in our organization?

What is the real product of my management team?

How do we produce leaders?

What's my process for battle-testing leaders before they've gone into battle?

How do we identify individuals that may have the potential to help us?

What is it about us that would cause top talent to work here?

What has been my most effective approach to attracting top talent? To retaining and engaging top talent?

Who are the stars? The under-performers? How do I motivate and reward the stars? How are under-performers addressed?

Can each employee tell me what constitutes a good result that they produce each day for the company?

How do I intend to approach succession planning? Have I committed any thoughts to paper to guide me through this process?

Customers + Prospects

"If you listen closely enough,
your customers will explain your
business to you."

Peter Schutz

Nothing happens in a business until somebody sells something. Being clear about what your customers and prospective customers value and then being clear about how you deliver that value can be the difference between a struggling business and a high-performing company. That clarity can also mark the difference between drudgery and fulfillment.

How have I strengthened customer relationships over the past 12 months?

When was the last time we reached out to our former customers? Is it possible that re-connecting with former customers would lead to doing business with them again? Who that we used to work with do I want to work with again?

What are the barriers customers and prospects must overcome to do business with us? What hurdles or barriers could we remove to make them major users? What reward can we provide them for taking the action we desire?

In our pursuit of new customers, have we structured responsibilities and activities to distinguish between marketing (which focuses on the 4 Ps – product, place [channel], price and promotion – that prepares the market for the sale) and sales (which is responsible for closing the deal)?

What's the risk of trying something new? What's the risk of not trying?

What are our customers asking for that we currently don't offer? What are our customers' unmet needs?

Who can we partner with that will allow us to extend our reach to our customers?

What memorable experience are we creating with our customers?

What is our "unfair" advantage that causes our customers to select us over our competition?

What are the characteristics of our best customers? What can we do to attract more of them?

What are the characteristics of our worst customers? What can we do to turn them into great customers? If we can't convert "bad" customers to "good" customers, what's our plan for firing them?

When we lose a "sale," what is typically the reason given by those selling? If I'm honest about it, what's the real reason we lose business opportunities?

In what situations is our company (or our products or services) discovered? Are there any surprising situations that represent an under-served opportunity? Who uses our product or service in a way that we did not intend for it to be used?

What is our customers' greatest pain? What would eliminating or reducing that pain be worth to customers? What might our solution look like? What resources of ours would be required? Would our solution give us an advantage? Would the victory be worth it?

Describe the most recent major breakthrough made at our company in terms of product, service or process. What has been the impact of that breakthrough?

Where will future profitable growth come from?

Which customers' needs are changing most significantly? What is driving this change? What opportunities do these changes present?

How would our customers describe our company? What would cause them to describe us in this way?

What do customers and prospects like most about our company? Least?

Do our customers or clients refer us to others? If yes, what can we do to increase these referrals? If no, what can we do to get them to start doing so?

Would I buy what we're selling?

Have we introduced a successful new product or service within the past 24 months?

What was the most creative sales or marketing idea we implemented in the past 12 months? What was its impact in revenue? In non-monetary ways?

Making Things Happen

"When it comes to getting things done, we need fewer architects and more bricklayers."

Colleen Barrett

When most companies and people fail to fully realize their dreams, it's not because the goal was unattainable or the approach to achieving it was flawed. Shortfalls generally occur because of the inability or unwillingness to maintain discipline and do the heavy lifting that's required.

Great companies share three characteristics: operational excellence, innovation and customization. Exceptional companies make one of these three their competitive advantage. With which do we lead?

How do I distinguish between an honest mistake and under-performance?

How are faster, better, cheaper ways of producing an intended result shared and replicated?

How well have we incented the behavior we want?

What single thing could I do this month to bring the most value to my company?

What area in my company do I most need to improve right now?

Do we measure the things that are important to us?

If what matters gets measured, what metrics do we have in place? What do they tell us?

Where is waste occurring in our organization?

What isn't working right in our organization?

How should our organization be structured to achieve the profitable growth we say we want? How does our ideal structure compare to the current organizational chart? Does our current organizational chart reflect the way work actually gets done?

Which of our current activities would we start now if they weren't already underway? What would be the impact if we began to eliminate anything not on the list?

Do I believe there's more than one way to skin a cat, or do I place value on the tried and true?

Am I open to multiple points of view or do I prefer examining an issue with people that think like me?

What's the most significant barrier to getting what I say I want? What am I going to do to overcome it?

Do I understand the difference between being comfortable and being effective?

What have I accomplished in the past 30 days?

Are we having fun? Am I having fun?

Personal Motivation

"I am always doing things I can't
do. That's how I get to do them."

Pablo Picasso

You're more likely to reach your goals if you're working from some type of written plan. But just because you have a plan doesn't mean things will always go your way. Stay focused on your goals and remember why they matter to you. You'll be better equipped to overcome obstacles, endure sacrifice and withstand setbacks as you press on toward realizing your dream.

What moment in my life most defines who I am today? Is it positive or negative? If it's negative, what must I change to become more of the person that I want to become? If it's positive, what else must I do to amplify that experience?

There are six major drivers that motivate us: money, power, order, harmony, learning, helping others. Which of these six drivers most motivates me?

What do I like about myself? What don't I like about myself? What am I willing to do to change this?

What does a perfect day look like for me? What can I do to enjoy more perfect days?

Would I agree to have dinner with myself? If so, would I enjoy it?

What in the past has brought me my greatest joy? What was it about these things that brought me joy? What have I done to replicate those things? What caused me to stop doing or pursuing the things that brought me this joy?

What in the past caused me anger, pain or frustration? To what extent am I still carrying this baggage? What can I do to leave that baggage behind?

What can I do to turn a breakdown into a breakthrough? When I'm feeling like the victim, what steps can I take to become the victor?

How do I recover from surprise? From disappointment?

What's my natural gift? How does my gift serve me? What turns my gift into a curse? When my gift becomes a curse, what does that cost me?

What am I afraid of?

How am I feeling today? What's driving this emotion?

What was the best moment for me in the last day? What made it special?

If I really believe that a good idea can come from anywhere, when was the last time I learned something from an unexpected source?

What boundaries have I set for myself? To what extent are these boundaries self-limiting beliefs that are simply holding me back? Do these self-limiting beliefs show up in certain situations more than others?

What is it that makes me feel grateful?

Change

"Everyone thinks of changing the world, but no one thinks of changing themselves."

Leo Tolstoy

Change is like surgery. If it's someone else's surgery, it's minor; if it's our own surgery, it's major. Either way, if something's not working, you can live with it or change it. If you decide to live with it, you allow forces mostly outside your influence to control your destiny. If you decide that change is called for, at least you're the one wielding the scalpel.

What is changing that excites me? That concerns me?

What's the biggest (and perhaps hardest) change I must make heading into the coming year? What's the biggest (and perhaps hardest) change the business must make?

What am I going to stop doing? Start doing? Continue doing? Finish doing?

Where am I stuck? Who can I turn to in order to get moving again?

If I was fired today, what changes would my replacement make? What's stopping me from making those changes now?

When I take an objective look at my business, what facts or trends jump out at me? To what factors do I attribute any upward or downward trends? How should these trends affect my long-term approach to the business?

Picture the worst. What's the impact of that result? What must I do to prevent this result from happening? What's stopping me from getting started today?

What factors does my industry take for granted that we should eliminate in our business?

What time-honored practices are no longer producing the desired results?

What are the most significant changes our competitors have made recently? How do those changes affect us? How will we choose to respond?

Can our current organizational structure support a new direction? What are the strengths of our organizational structure? How are these strengths being replicated and reinforced?

Will our business – on its current trajectory – enable me achieve my personal goals? If not, what change must occur in order to get where I say I want to go?

How do I distinguish from having convictions about an idea, person or issue versus being stubborn or inflexible?

What's the most difficult criticism for me to accept?

What are my best habits? My worst? Which habit do I want to become more intentional about emphasizing? Which habit is holding me back? What must I do to change, minimize, or – better yet – eliminate that bad habit?

If I could do it again, what would I do differently?

Accountability

"When all is said and done, more is
said than done."

Lou Holtz

Mistakes happen. Under-performance is a pattern. So when things don't get done, remember that you get the behavior you're willing to tolerate. How you address under-performance says as much about you as it does the person not meeting expectations.

What contract am I willing to make with myself to hold myself to my commitment?

How can we articulate this goal in a way that we'll be able to look back on it and either say, "We did it" or "We didn't"?

What promises do we make as an organization that we have difficulty keeping? What's the impact of breaking these promises?

If I were to ask my colleagues for ways to consistently keep our promises, what would they say? What would they tell me that I must do as a leader to create a culture of accountability?

As colleagues, how well do we keep our promises to one another? What would be the impact of doing what we said we would do when we said we would do it? How much is not practicing this behavior costing us now?

Have I been clear in my expectations – of myself as well as of others – or are my emotions getting in the way?

When expectations are clear yet the expectations are not being met, is the underperformance occurring because of lack of skill or lack of will?

If the expectations are clear and the leaders on my team have agreed to hold one another accountable, what should I be expected to say or do about the underperformance that's occurring?

Whose job am I doing today?

To what extent do my personal issues color my view of performance, whether it's my performance or someone else's?

If an employee fails at a task, do they know where to go for help?

How long can the organization accept the impact of underperformance?

What's keeping me from having a tough conversation with an under-performer?

Before having a tough conversation about performance, I should ask myself these questions: Is the under-performer willing to change? Will he or she hear what I'm saying? Will my feedback help? How much of myself am I willing to invest in helping this under-performer get back on track?

Results

"It is an immutable law in business that words are words, explanations are explanations, promises are promises but only performance is reality."

Harold Geneen

At the beginning of the day, it's all about possibilities. At the end of a day, a year or a life, it's all about having accomplished the things that matter most to you. What are those things?

I've lived a rich, full life. It's over and friends and relatives have gathered to celebrate my life. What's being said about me in the eulogy?

If I died today and had written a letter to a board of advisors about my business, what would the letter say? Is there anything that's keeping me from writing that letter today?

I'm picturing my greatest achievement. What must happen to top it?

What were my personal significant accomplishments of the past year?

What were my personal significant disappointments of the past year?

What were my company's most significant accomplishments of the past year?

What were my company's most significant disappointments of the past year?

Am I getting what I signed up for? What I expect? What I deserve?

If the expectations I set are appropriate yet they're not being met, what's causing the gap between my expectations and the actual performance?

What's the first step I must take to change the results I'm getting to the results I want?

What will happen if the obstacles in the way of my goal are not removed?

What's at least one good thing that can come out of a particular bad situation?

Are those I work with having fun doing what we're doing? Am I?

Are we committed to winning? How can I tell?

What are the systems we've put in place to measure the things that are important to us?

How am I rewarding those that helped me accomplish my objectives? How am I addressing those that are holding me back?

What advice should I have given myself three years ago?

What's my magic number? Do my business partners or investors agree? Does my life partner?

Who am I being that is causing the results that I'm getting?

Blue Sky

"It's kind of fun to do the impossible."

Walt Disney

The human mind is a remarkable tool. It constructs roadblocks that don't exist, and imagines possibilities previously unseen. So free your mind, allow it to soar and fly along with it to a new destination.

What career do I secretly wish I was qualified for?

If there were no constraints, what would I do?

If I had only 24 hours to live, how would I live it? One year? What am I waiting for?

If I could change one thing about the world what would it be? What first step can I take to help bring about this change?

If I could change my company, what would it be? What's stopping me from taking a step toward that change?

If I held a dinner party and could invite any person alive or dead, who would it be and why? What question would I most like to ask them?

If I could go back and meet myself as a 12-year-old, what would I say?

If my house was burning, what are the five objects I'd make sure got out with me?

If I had it to do over again – let's say I was just starting out – what would I do differently?

What would I do if I had no money worries?

What would I do if I didn't work?

What basic assumptions am I making about my future and what's possible for me?

Just for Fun

"Today was good. Today was fun.

Tomorrow is another one."

Dr. Seuss

Approach the world with a child's curiosity, imagination and innocence and startling possibilities emerge. Answer these brain tinglers for yourself when you're alone, then the next time you're in a group setting – a meeting, for instance – select a question and ask it to help break the ice and unleash imaginations. You may be surprised by the serious impact of a whimsical question.

If every day was a Saturday, what would I do?

If I had a million dollars, what would I do?

If I had a magic wand, how would I use it?

Do I ever dream with my eyes open? What's my daytime dream?

If I found $1,000 in a vacant lot, what would I do?

What's a secret about me that would surprise those that think they know me well?

If I were a color, what color would I be? What's the story?

What does my handwriting say about me?

If I were to come back in life, what would I be?

When I was little, what did I want to be when I grew up? Is there still time?

If every time I entered the room a song was played, what would that song be?

What's been the best day of my life?

If I played a sport, what sport would I choose? What position would I play? What does this say about me?

Who would I most like to meet?

If I could be anyone in the world for a day, who would I like to be? What's the story behind my choice?

If I won the Nobel Prize, what would I have done to deserve it?

Asking Great Questions

"I have no special talent. I am only passionately curious."

Albert Einstein

When sitting down with another person to ask them questions about themselves, it's worth knowing what you're both trying to accomplish.

The very first session for a person that's never worked with a coach or had a serious conversation focused on self-discovery and self-improvement can be a bit awkward. The person on the receiving end of the questions will want to know how the session is supposed to work, what they should say, and what outcome should be expected.

I try to keep things simple and generally set only three ground rules.

Establishing ground rules

The first rule is confidentiality. The person I'm coaching must trust absolutely that's what said between us will go no farther – not to a board member, a fellow owner, a colleague or even a spouse.

A second ground rule is that the person must be willing to do the work that will be the by-product of our sessions. A coach can't make a person want to succeed – that comes from within. As coaching great Lou Holtz said, "Ability is what you're capable of doing. Motivation determines what you do. Attitude determines how well you do it."

A third ground rule is based on the understanding that the conversation may at times be uncomfortable. I get permission in advance to ask one more question when there's reluctance to answer an uncomfortable question. *"What is it about that question that causes discomfort?"*

Beyond that, I tell them that the time is theirs to use to their advantage.

Setting expectations

People turn to coaches for a variety of reasons, and these are the five primary ones that I've seen:

- **Self development** – A good coach will ask questions that expose the blind spots we all have. We're simply oblivious to certain issues, situations, people or even our own actions that others see all too clearly or in a completely different light. Socrates used questions to illuminate core truths. "Know thyself," Socrates said, noting that self-knowledge is the starting point for self development.

- **Sounding board** – A confidential session with a trusted advisor is like a laboratory where you can experiment with new ideas and try them out or discuss them to see if they appear viable before implementing them in your business or personal life. In this setting, it's okay to make mistakes, admit fear and wrestle with uncertainty. Even when you think you know the answer, a confidential session with a person you trust is a great place to have your answers questioned.

- **Outlet for steam** – It is indeed lonely at the top, and sometimes the executives I coach have no one else to turn to in order to simply blow off steam. *"I can't talk about* *this with my board." "My spouse just doesn't understand, and I don't want to worry him/her with this stuff." "I'm so disappointed with our business performance, I'm considering firing three of my five direct reports." "My business partner and I no longer see eye-to-eye on the company's future direction."* You may be surprised how cathartic it can be to unload your burden to someone who cares, knowing that your secret's safe with them. What's more, you'll find that a solution usually emerges.

- **Resource repository** – When a decision's been made, the executive sometimes requires the help of specialists to implement his or her decision. Whether it's a tax specialist or valuation expert, sales consultant or marketing guru, psychological therapist or marriage counselor, a good coach usually has plenty of independent resources in mind that are willing to visit with the executive in a separate conversation about whether or not they can be helpful.

- **Accountability partner** – The person I'm working with commits to taking action on one or more issues that emerge from our session. We use a two-part carbonless form. The executive writes down the action he or she will take, and then I get the top copy and they keep the bottom copy. Knowing that there's a deadline – specifically, that I'll be asking about those action items at our next session – is usually enough to make things happen. As my wife Janet says, "If you want to get something done around the house, have a party." For the executives I'm coaching, that party is always just around the corner.

Getting started

In my coaching sessions, we generally spend only a few minutes on initial pleasantries. I like to get into the real reason we're there – to help the person I'm coaching dig into the issues that are important to them. We typically spend 90 minutes to two hours together during each session, and most of these sessions occur every month, sometimes more frequently if there's a specific issue we're working on.

Here are five sure-fire sets of conversation starters (you may recognize some of these from previous sections):

1. What's the most important thing we should be talking about today? (Sometimes, this initial question is the basis for the entire session.)

2. What isn't working right in your organization? Your life? What's causing this?

3. What's the most important long-term opportunity for your company? What could you be doing about it this month?

4. What commitments did you make at our last coaching session? How are you doing on those commitments?

5. How are you doing on your personal plan for the year (the 7 Fs)?

You'll certainly bring your own questions, and the conversation will prompt more. These five form the foundation of every single coaching session I conduct.

Giving a good coaching session

From the more than 1,600 executive coaching sessions I've conducted, I've learned that the differences between a good session and a really great one are as fundamental as A-B-C-D-E.

So whether you're asking questions of yourself or someone else, remember to apply these five essential components:

Authentic Advocacy – Start with a genuine desire to help the person accomplish something that matters to them and your belief that they can do it. You can treat the process as you would a conversation with a good friend or you may find that it's more appropriate to approach the session as a doctor with a patient. Either way, it's critical as noted previously to establish ground rules for tackling meaty issues. All the while, the intention behind the question must be honorable, not judgmental. You're seeking to expose blind spots that may be hindering good decision-making and constraining performance. If trust is absent and the conditions for an honest exchange are not agreed upon, you'll ask lightweight questions that generate lightweight answers.

Bring your Best – Armed with an attitude of advocacy, bring a couple of key questions you want to ask, such as those noted above. But bring more than that. Bring your undivided attention. Prepare to be a patient, active listener. When you're fully present – not thinking about something else in your busy life or what you'll say next – you'll become completely engaged in what the other person is trying to tell you. Or avoid telling you. You owe them your "A" game as they begin to talk about their hopes, fears and uncertainties. In our microwave society where everything is fast, fast, fast and we "talk" through technology, giving another human being our complete attention is one of the greatest gifts they'll ever receive.

Curiosity Counts – As you listen to the other person talk, pay careful attention to their choice of words. Ask for elaboration when you hear a word or phrase that's loaded with meaning or when one set of words contradicts another. Listen for what's not being said. Watch body language. These are clues for the next question. Closed-ended questions that ask *When* and *Who* and for *Yes* or *No* answers have their place; open-ended questions that ask *What* or *How* help people open up because those kinds of questions require description and may have multiple answers. So be curious. Ask the dumb question, the obvious question, the tough question, the playful question, the unexpected question. Asking these types of questions changes the paradigm of a person's mindset and may help them confront their self-limiting beliefs or consider the issue from a fresh perspective. You are their catalyst for self-observation. So resist the temptation to answer for them. Make them work for the answer. Don't let them off the hook. The trick is knowing when to hug and when to kick.

Dig Deep – Sometimes, the first answer to a question is not the ultimate answer. When you sense the answer you're getting is a surface answer, ask again. One method for digging deeply into an issue is to repeat back an answer in the form of a question.

Another method was first developed by Sakichi Toyoda and later employed by the Toyota Motor Company. It's called "The Five Why's" from the practice of asking, five times, why a failure has occurred or a belief is held in order to drill down to the root cause or causes of a problem, opportunity or issue. *Why* is a powerful word. When asked in the context of choices a person has made, it can trigger a defensive response (we'll look at more of these words later). Some of this defensiveness stems from the four fatal fears we all carry around: Failure, rejection, being wrong, emotional discomfort. When you encounter one of these fears, circle back to the ground rules you established and ask one more time. As you frame the question, remember that you're not interrogating a witness. You're there to help.

Exit and Execution – Ask for and get a commitment from the person to act on the decisions they've made as a result of answering the questions during the conversation. Ask them to write down the actions they will take with deadlines and desired outcomes. When you've done that, your job is done. You exit. You can and should hold them accountable. The execution is up to the person that has committed to changing. Not you.

Seven words to watch

There are seven words that have the power to trigger emotionally charged reactions and create responses that are unintended.

111

We just mentioned that *Why* can be viewed by some people in certain contexts as a word that's judgmental.

Here's one example: If you ask someone, for instance, *"Why do you believe this behavior is wrong?"* your question could be interpreted as accusatory. The person may feel as though you're attacking their belief system, questioning their ability to distinguish right from wrong, disagreeing with their point of view or a dozen other things that could put them on the defensive. If, on the other hand, you frame your question as *"How have you come to believe this behavior is wrong?"* you're interested in understanding the story behind the statement.

Here's another example. Avoid asking, *"Why didn't you accomplish the action items that you committed to completing at our last session?"* That's an accusation along the lines of *"Where were you on the night of the 23rd?"* Try another approach. Sometimes, the best question isn't even a question. *"Tell me what prevented last month's priorities from being completed."* Now it's a conversation and you're listening for clues about what's really going on. By the way, this approach eliminates two of the seven judgmental words used in the previous question.

Please understand that I'm not suggesting that you sugarcoat questions, nor am I advising you to pull punches or speak in politically correct language when asking questions. I'm simply reporting that my experience has been that these seven words can trigger a response that causes the person on the receiving end of that question to shut down instead of open up.

Here are the seven words:

You

Your

Always

Never

Should

But

Why

Avoid asking questions that start with *You* or *Your* – you might as well be pointing an accusing finger at the person. Practice framing open-ended questions and consider ways of asking *What* or *How* in place of the other more judgmental words.

Your imagination is fertile enough that you can see how the words above could be viewed as offensive and cause the person on the receiving end to put up their guard.

Asking great questions is about keeping things simple – though that doesn't always mean it's easy. Asking great questions is more than a checklist. It's a conversation. A dance.

So remember that none of these guidelines is a foolproof method for asking great questions.

They're a start, and they're ones that have worked for me.

One Last Question

"No question is so difficult to answer as that to which the answer is obvious."

George Bernard Shaw

You find yourself at the end of a book filled with provocative questions.

You've answered most, if not all, of them.

Through the process of answering these questions, you've been prompted to think about issues you may not have previously considered in a meaningful way in order to come to grips with what's really important to you.

Having accomplished this, you're now prepared to take action and commit to enhancing your life.

So there's just one last question to answer.

Now what?

68571676R00080

Made in the USA
Middletown, DE
16 September 2019